NEW ROADS BY NEW MEANS

--BRINGING IN PRIVATE FINANCE--

A CONSULTATION PAPER

Presented to Parliament by the Secretary of State for Transport by Command of Her Majesty
May 1989

LONDON
HER MAJESTY'S STATIONERY OFFICE

Cm 698   £3.10 net

Cover Photograph:
Artist's Impression of the
Dartford - Thurrock Bridge

FOREWORD

This Government has shown time and again that pushing back the boundaries of the public sector gives a better service to customers and a better deal to taxpayers. Transport is no exception: already the private sector is playing an important, and growing, role in providing transport infrastructure. From the international partnership on the Channel Tunnel to local partnerships with councils on road schemes, the initiative and flair of the private sector are making their impression.

I believe that still more of our roads and bridges can be financed privately. The Dartford-Thurrock Bridge - the first private road scheme this century - is our starting point. There is a reservoir of potential which I and my colleagues are determined to tap so that the private sector can play its part in giving Britain a modern transport infrastructure.

Michael Portillo and I have talked to many people about our ideas. We have found much enthusiasm but, as with all new ideas, a number of questions too. In this paper, we seek to answer these questions. We recognise that the success of privately financed road schemes depends upon speedy and unhindered procedures. But we are sure that this must not be at the expense of the environment, the rights of individuals or the safety of road users.

This is a consultation document. We want to hear your views. With your help, we shall find the right way forward.

PAUL CHANNON

CONSULTATION PAPER ON PRIVATE FINANCE FOR ROADS

INTRODUCTION

1. The Government wishes to encourage greater private sector involvement in the provision of roads. This consultation paper proposes new procedures for authorising privately financed roads. It seeks comments on these new procedures and other policy and procedural aspects of private finance for roads. It covers Great Britain.

OBJECTIVES

2. The Government's objective is to harness the entrepreneurial, financial and management skills of the private sector to the provision of roads. Trunk road construction is done in the private sector. The Department employs no direct labour. The great majority of detailed planning, design and supervision is done by private sector consultants. Now the aim is to extend the role of the private sector in the promotion, finance and operation of roads. Such roads, built, financed and operated using efficient and competitive methods, will add to and complement the existing and proposed public network.

3. The Government is looking for genuine private sector ventures, with appropriate risks and rewards. There is no place for financial devices, disguised Government borrowing or guarantees. Shadow tolls, for example, where the Government makes payments to the private sector operator according to the number of vehicles using the road, are ruled out for this reason.

PROGRESS SO FAR

4. A great deal of transport infrastructure is already being developed by the private sector. The fact that the private sector is financing and building, and will operate, the Channel Tunnel shows that it can undertake the largest and most complex schemes. In addition the extension to the Docklands Light Railway is being partly funded by the developers of Canary Wharf; the new rail link to Heathrow is being financed largely by the private sector; BR has invited the private sector to participate in the proposed rail link to the Channel tunnel; and private firms are bidding to design, build, operate and maintain the proposed light rail system in Manchester.

5. The Dartford-Thurrock Bridge, now under construction, is being designed, built and financed by the private sector, and will be operated by them for the life of the concession. Private sector firms are also bidding to design, build, finance and operate the second Severn bridge. Many smaller road projects associated with property developments are being funded by the private sector. The Government wishes to tap to the full the potential for the private sector to undertake more road projects both large and small.

ROADS FINANCED BY DEVELOPERS

6. For road safety and traffic reasons it is necessary to limit the number and siting of accesses to trunk roads, and other primary traffic routes. However, where a developer is proposing a major development in the vicinity of such a road, it may be possible, depending on the circumstances, for agreement to be made with the Secretary of State or the local highway authority whereby the developer funds in whole or part the cost of the works needed to accommodate the traffic effects of the development. These arrangements benefit the community by allowing beneficial development to proceed, while maintaining, and even, in some cases, improving traffic flow. The developer for his part gains by the removal of traffic objections to his development, and by making it more attractive. Of course contributions to highway improvements cannot make acceptable developments that are unacceptable for other reasons.

7. Increasing numbers of road schemes are being financed in this way. On trunk roads alone some 50 agreements have been concluded since April 1986 and another 50 are at an advanced stage of preparation. Many more schemes are being undertaken on local roads; local highway authorities are increasingly getting considerable contributions from developers towards by-passes, relief roads and other improvements.

8. These projects are welcome when they enhance the capacity of the network for general road users. The Government has issued guidance (Department of Transport Circular 1/89: Welsh Office Circular 13/89) to ensure that developers are aware of the possibilities, to clarify the procedures applying in such cases and to help reduce the time taken to reach agreements.

9. Agreements with the Secretary of State in respect of trunk road schemes can be made under the powers in S.278 of the Highways Act 1980. S.278 is also available to local highway authorities. The Government proposes to introduce legislation as soon as Parliamentary time permits to facilitate new roads financed by developers. Subject to the approval of Parliament the legislation will provide new powers for the building by a highway authority of a highway partly or wholly funded by a private developer with contributions by the developer for maintenance. It will give related compulsory purchase powers to the highway authority in appropriate circumstances. The procedures for the taking over by a highway authority as a highway a road which has been built by a developer would also be simplified.

10. Most agreements for developer-financed schemes on local authority roads are covered by the powers in S.52 of the Town and Country Planning Act 1971. These powers appear to be adequate, and the Government has no similar plans to amend S.52.

TOLLED ROADS

11. The other principal way of paying for a privately financed road is some form of toll. The remainder of the proposals in this consultation paper are concerned with tolled roads.

ISSUES ON PRIVATELY FINANCED TOLLED ROADS

12. Private firms interested in financing and building tolled roads will need to know the framework within which they are operating. They will need to be confident that there are proper procedures in place to enable such schemes to be developed before they will commit finance and resources to a project. The Government has already had some discussions with a number of firms and has considered the points which they have raised. The following section represents the Government's current thinking on these issues on which further comments are invited.

VIABILITY

13. To be viable a tolled road must provide some advantage over other untolled routes for which road users would be prepared to pay. Estuarial crossings generally offer a significant time saving for the motorist since they usually provide the only direct route. In the right circumstances, such routes can be successfully tolled.

14. In other busy transport corridors, congestion itself can form a barrier to traffic, rather like an estuary. Some road users will be prepared to pay to avoid congested sections of road. One possible application of private finance would therefore be a new route which offered significant benefits in terms of avoiding congestion and for which enough people were willing to pay to finance the scheme.

15. Such schemes might include roads access to which was limited to particular groups of vehicles. For example, lanes for cars only have been suggested. In areas where many road users have a high value of time this could be a profitable venture for the private sector. Car only lanes might also be attractive to many motorists as they could provide a less stressful environment for drivers, as well as saving time. HGV only lanes might also be a possibility.

16. There is no way of saying in advance how many or which privately financed toll roads would be viable. Only the market can decide that, and once a tolled road is constructed, the market will decide whether it is a commercial success.

STATUS OF SCHEMES

17. The Government's view is that privately financed roads should be an integral part of the national highway network, and that the road traffic regulation legislation should apply to them as it does to other roads; anything else would be confusing to road users and probably dangerous. The Secretary of State will therefore be the "highway authority" though many of the highway authority's functions and duties will be delegated to the private operator who will finance the road and collect the tolls.

18. The arrangements will rest on new statutory procedures (see below) and on the terms of a concession or lease granted by the Secretary of State to the promoter.

PROCEDURES

19. Present procedures for authorising roads in the Highways Act 1980 are designed for schemes constructed by the Secretary of State (trunk roads) or by local highway authorities. They are not appropriate to tolled roads constructed by the private sector. In addition all tolls need specific statutory authorisation.

20. The practical consequence is that privately financed roads at present have to be authorised individually by Act of Parliament.

21. The Hybrid Bill procedure was used to authorise the Dartford-Thurrock Bridge. This process - building on the precedent of the Channel Tunnel - involves:

- the identification by the Government of a corridor for the proposed road;

- a competition for the financing, building and operation of a road serving that corridor, inviting bids from private firms;

- the award by the Government of a concession to the winner;

- the promotion by the Government of a Hybrid Bill to authorise the road, the tolls, land acquisition and arrangements for the concession.

22. The Government may use this Hybrid Bill procedure again. Private promoters also have the option of a private bill. But Parliamentary time is limited, and since for other highways an alternative authorisation procedure is regularly used, the Government has concluded that the authorisation of privately financed roads by individual Acts of Parliament should be supplemented by a new procedure.

A NEW PROCEDURE

23. A procedure for privately financed schemes would need to :

- establish as speedy a process as possible;

- safeguard the environment and the rights of individuals affected by proposals to build roads;

- place the appropriate responsibility for promotion on the private sector;

- avoid the need for a Bill for each scheme.

24. A procedure to authorise a privately financed toll road could be :-

   (1) either - a private sector road promoter would decide on his own initiative that a particular route was technically feasible and likely to attract sufficient toll-paying business (supplemented perhaps by contributions from unlocked development potential or privately acquired land) to be profitable. The Government would decide whether a competition was needed in the light of the circumstances. In most cases, a competition would be required for the reasons set out in paragraph 27 below

   or - the Secretary of State would identify a corridor - usually not a detailed proposal - and invite competitive bids from would-be promoters for that corridor

   (2) following any competition, the promoter would ask the Secretary of State to make the Line Order to authorise the construction of the road, and to enter into the necessary concession agreement with him, including arrangements for tolls. The promoter would consult with Government, local planning and highway authorities, local people etc. before making that application. The application for the Line Order should include information such as the standard, general design features, lighting and environmental effects

   (3) the Secretary of State would have discretion whether to allow the application to proceed. Clearly he would not take further some types of applications, for example because of their environmental effects, their effects on the existing road network or because the proposal was simply not feasible. The Secretary of State might also decide that the proposal had not been developed adequately. He might then ask the promoter to work the proposal up further

   (4) if he decided to proceed and there were any relevant objections the Secretary of State would set up a public inquiry at which the promoter would present the case for his proposals. If there were no objections and therefore no public inquiry the promoter would still have to consult the public on the Environmental Statement

   (5) the promoter would prepare an Environmental Statement when required by the regulations implementing the European Directive on environmental assessment or by the relevant guidelines. There would be public consultation on this document before any public inquiry, but the Statement would be considered at the inquiry in any event

(6) on the basis of the inquiry the Secretaries of State for Transport and the Environment would decide whether or not to make the Order with or without amendment. Clearly some amendments would not be acceptable to the promoter and would amount to an effective refusal

(7) the promoter would have to make proposals acceptable to the Secretary of State and any relevant local highway authority for linking the proposed road to existing ones. The cost of such links would be borne by the promoter, and he would have to come to an agreement with the local highway authority as to their operation, maintenance etc. Any Orders required to cross or stop-up a local road, navigable watercourse or private right of way would be considered at the public inquiry, as would any need for other powers eg to discharge surface water to drainage systems

(8) if the promoter were unable to acquire all the land he required for the construction of the road he would ask the Secretary of State for Transport to exercise compulsory purchase powers on his behalf, if the Secretary of State agreed that the scheme was in the public interest and the land was necessary for it. Only the owner or occupier of the land in question should be able to object to such a Compulsory Purchase Order, which would be heard at the same public inquiry as the objections to the Line Order. Compensation for compulsory purchase would be on the normal terms of the compensation code

(9) the Line Order or another Order considered at the same inquiry would authorise the charging of tolls, and set out the tolling regime

(10) having received these various approvals the promoter would construct, finance, operate and maintain the road.

25. Subject to comments on these proposals the Government proposes to introduce legislation at the earliest opportunity to adapt the Highways Act 1980 to authorise these procedures.

EXCLUSIVITY

26. It is sometimes argued that private sector promoters should enjoy "exclusive" rights to schemes. This would mean either:

(1) that the Government should enter into an exclusive arrangement with one private sector promoter to facilitate a scheme, without that scheme being subject to competition; or

(2) that the private sector promoter should enjoy the benefit of having first thought of a scheme or innovation if the scheme is eventually undertaken by another firm, eg by financial compensation.

It is argued that without such arrangements no one will propose a road because of the risks of abortive expenditure and preparation.

27. The Government understands these concerns, though experience so far does not suggest that the flow of ideas and bids from the private sector will dry up without exclusivity. The Government's main concern is that the market should play as full a part as possible, with a particular emphasis on competition helping to keep tolls to the road user down. Where the Government is supporting a promoter by compulsory purchase (see para 36) or hybrid legislation, it would wish to be able to point to the results of a competition to justify its support for a particular option. Competitions for concessions are also required by the draft EC Directive on the co-ordination of procedures for the award of public works contracts, which follows in this respect the Declaration of 26 July 1971 of the representatives of the Governments of the Member States. Therefore where privately financed roads take the form of a concession under Community law competitions will be required.

28. The Government believes that it would not be practical to devise a formal system to compensate a firm which claimed to have originated an idea or proposal which was eventually undertaken by another firm. But where Government itself held a competition and there was a prima facie case that a firm had initiated an idea, the Government would ensure that it had a place on the short list; and, having done preparatory work, it could be in a strong position. Commercially confidential innovations would not be disclosed by the Government or used as the basis for competitions.

TOLLS

29. Motorists will pay to use roads only if the benefits to them outweigh the costs. Therefore promoters will make money only if they provide a good service at a reasonable level of tolls. So the market could to some extent determine the level of tolls. Views are sought on the extent to which further controls should be imposed on toll levels and increases.

30. The Government's view is that where a monopoly, such as an estuarial crossing, is built it will probably be necessary for the Government to impose some form of control on the level of the toll to be charged and on the rate at which that toll can be increased. Any regime agreed in the concession will be included in the tolling Order and amended by Order as appropriate.

31. Monopolies of this kind are few, and are very different from tolled, privately financed roads in competition for road users against nearby public roads which are free at the point of use. Here the motorist can make a reasoned choice either to pay for the improved facility or to use other roads. In such a case it should not be necessary for the Government to seek to limit the level of tolls or the rate of increase in tolls. It would be up to the promoter to charge a toll which attracted the level of custom which he required. A variable toll, charged at different rates at different times of day, is not ruled out. If the toll rate were not competitive the scheme would fail.

THE ENVIRONMENT

32. A privately financed road scheme would have to comply with the same environmental requirements as a Government scheme. The Department of Transport takes great care to minimise the effect of its road schemes on the environment. Consultations are extensive and both the selection of a line and the detailed design of the roads are heavily influenced by environmental considerations. Construction is almost always accompanied by extensive landscaping and planting. If the Secretary of State were not satisfied that the promoter had applied similarly high standards to his proposal the scheme would not be approved. The promoter would, as part of the concession, have a duty to maintain landscaping works.

33. If a road fell within the criteria of the EC Directive on Environmental Impact Assessment or the Department of Transport's guidelines a full Environmental Statement in line with the requirements of the Directive would have to be prepared. The Directive requires that the public have an opportunity to comment. Even if no public inquiry were needed, consultation on the environmental effects of the scheme would still have to take place.

34. A promoter would also be expected to conform to existing Government procedures for publicly financed roads in the provision of noise insulation and compensation for those adversely affected by proposals for and the construction and operation of the privately financed road.

LAND ACQUISITION

35. A promoter might well be able to acquire the land needed for the road by negotiation as for an ordinary private development. It is, however, probable that with a linear development of this sort there will be some landowners who will hold the promoter to ransom seeking higher and higher prices for their land, while others may simply wish to delay or prevent the construction of the road.

36. In such a situation a promoter could not complete a scheme for which he had otherwise obtained full approval. The Secretary of State must be in a position to exercise his compulsory purchase powers to support the scheme if necessary and if he believes the project to be in the public interest. It may also be appropriate to use them for the provision of services to road users, where necessary in accordance with Departmental policies and standards. It would be for the promoter to prove that the land was required in connection with the road, and safeguards would be needed to ensure compliance with these policies and standards. The Secretary of State would not exercise his compulsory purchase powers for purely commercial ventures associated with the road. Compulsory purchase by the Secretary of State on behalf of the promoter would be at market rates assessed by the District Valuer, as it is for new public roads, and the promoter would reimburse the Secretary of State. It would be open to the promoter to pay more to acquire land voluntarily.

OPERATION OF THE ROAD

37. As proposed above, privately financed roads will be roads for which the Secretary of State is highway authority and which he "leases out" to the private operator. Traffic regulation and similar powers will remain with the Secretary of State.

38. The law relating to road traffic includes requirements relating to the type approval, construction, maintenance and use of vehicles, the driving and operation of vehicles and insurance. The law relating to traffic regulation includes speed limits, prohibitions and restrictions on parking, halting, direction of flow, and temporary closures. This law is contained in primary and secondary legislation. It is proposed that the law on both road traffic and road traffic regulation should apply to the privately financed roads authorised by the procedures described here.

39. It may be necessary to amend the primary legislation to allow for certain special provisions relating to some privately financed roads or to allow the Secretary of State to make adaptations by order, where safety was not compromised, to meet the needs of the operators' business for example to restrict the use of roads to particular classes of vehicles.

40. The roads will be highways and highway law will apply to them. However, it may be desirable to amend the primary legislation so as to enable the Secretary of State as the highway authority to recover from the commercial undertaking the cost of his liabilities, and for the undertaking to provide indemnities.

GUARANTEES

41. There will be no Government financial guarantees.

42. Because of the Secretary of State's statutory duties under the Highways Act, the Government could not give an absolute guarantee not to build a road which would compete with a privately funded road, although some limited guarantees might be given. Such guarantees would be along the lines of those used for the Dartford-Thurrock Bridge where the Government has undertaken for a period not to construct or authorise a further crossing within a certain distance up or downstream of the bridge, subject to the Secretary of State's over-riding statutory duties.

REVERSION

43. Existing privately financed transport projects will revert to the State at the end of the concession period. An example is the Dartford-Thurrock Bridge. In that case the decision was taken in the belief that it would be wrong for a private undertaking, after the debt had been extinguished, to make high profits on a piece of public infrastructure and that it was more appropriate, where the compulsory acquisition of land was concerned, for the facility to return to the State, rather than that the private undertaking should own it in perpetuity and be able to dispose of it in whatever way it thought fit. The Government is disposed to maintain the practice that the assets should revert to the State: the length of the period of the concession and the terms of reversion would depend on the circumstances in each case.

ADDITIONALITY

44. There has been much misunderstanding about additionality. Many have claimed that privately funded schemes must be additional to those funded by the Exchequer if private finance is to attract the construction industry (which would wish to see an increase in its business overall) or the road user (who wants more roads, not just differently financed ones). But the annual level of expenditure on the road programme is determined by the Government in the light of the economy generally and the needs of that programme; a different method of financing it does not make more resources available. The private financing of a scheme already in the road programme, and for which public expenditure resources have been allocated, will not free that public expenditure for other projects. For these reasons the Government, in roads as in other fields (such as housing), has to take account of the provision being made by the private sector in considering the size of its public sector programme. But it is not practical - the timescales are wrong - in the great majority of cases to decide whether individual schemes are additional or not. The Government therefore gives the assurance that it will not subtract privately financed roads from public sector provision on a scheme-by-scheme basis. The Government believes that in practice private sector schemes will provide the opportunity for more roads than would otherwise have been built.

COMPARISONS WITH PUBLIC SECTOR OPTIONS

45. The Government is concerned to achieve the most cost-effective provision of roads. In the case of the Dartford-Thurrock Bridge it compared the costs and benefits of private sector provision with the public sector alternative. This comparison will also be applied to the second Severn Bridge. Such a comparison makes sense where there is a realistic public sector alternative, and will continue to be used in such circumstances. But there are drawbacks where there is no realistic public sector alternative, and promoters would be put off. The Government therefore intends to adopt as a working assumption that no comparison with public sector alternatives will be made unless such a scheme is in the programme or where there is a high degree of monopoly as in estuarial crossings such as Dartford and the Severn.

46. Where any such comparisons are made, the Government will make every effort to ensure that the costs and risks of both public and private sector options are fairly assessed.

GOVERNMENT PROPOSALS FOR AN EARLY COMPETITION

47. The Government does not have the monopoly of ideas for possible routes and corridors which might be appropriate for privately funded roads. Other groups, including local authorities, are already investigating the feasibility of particular schemes. The East Coast Motorway is one example. For its part the Government proposes to establish an early competition for a privately financed scheme to increase road capacity broadly in the corridor between Birmingham and Manchester.

LOCAL HIGHWAY AUTHORITIES

48. The Secretary of State will not be restricted to authorising and being highway authority for roads which, if they were publicly financed, would be trunk roads. Nevertheless, some roads proposed by private promoters will be of mainly local importance. Views are invited as to whether it would be useful to have provisions in any legislation so that local highway authorities could perform a similar role to the Secretary of State in relation to such proposals.

SCOTLAND

49. Road schemes financed by developers have been growing in Scotland as elsewhere in Britain. About 20 such schemes on the trunk road network are under discussion currently, many at an advanced stage, and most of these relate to grade separated junctions to provide safe and convenient access to valuable or potentially valuable development sites. The Government welcomes these projects when they enhance the capacity of the network for general road users and they are beneficial and proper in planning terms. Subject to the approval of Parliament, the Government proposes to amend the Roads (Scotland) Act 1984 to provide equivalent powers to those being proposed in England and Wales for S.278 of the Highways Act 1980. The powers in section 50 of the Town and Country Planning (Scotland) Act 1972 appear to be adequate for local authority roads and the Government has no plans to amend the Act.

50. There will from time to time be ad hoc opportunities in Scotland for privately financed schemes funded through tolls. For example, interest has been expressed by construction firms in the possibility of a privately financed bridge to Skye. The Government is willing to discuss with the private sector opportunities for privately funded schemes in Scotland and proposes that the new procedures described in this paper should equally be applied to Scotland.

PERIOD FOR CONSULTATION

51. Comments should be sent to Mr P.E. Pickering, Room P3/052, 2 Marsham Street, London SW1P 3EB, by 14 July 1989.